AS I REMEMBER

BY

W. EUGENE SWEENEY

To Lenore,
Hope you enjoy reading a little about my life.

Gene Sweeney
8/30/16

DEDICATION

This book is dedicated to my wife Lorraine, for devoting many hours to assist me in creating this book of memories and making a lifelong dream come true. I'd also like to thank the Writer's Club at the Morningside Library for all their help and support.

Copyright 2016 W. Eugene Sweeney

All rights reserved. No part of this book may be reproduced in any form or by any means, electronic, mechanical, recording or otherwise, without the written permission of W. Eugene Sweeney.

Cover by Pamela Frost
Digital formatting by
Scatteredfrost Publishing
Your Book Your Way
www.scatteredfrost.com

ISBN-13: 978-1533502391
ISBN-10: 1533502390

TABLE OF CONTENTS

SECTION I
THE MILITARY LIFE

World War II Scrap Drive	10
Pearl Harbor	13
Look Back at D-Day	14
Working During World War II	15
VE Day	18
V-J Day	19
USMCR	21
Prince Charles	23
Marching off to War	25
Hardest Thing	27
The Med Cruise	29
Nice, France	31
Sergeant of Guard Duty	32
Accidental Shooting	33
Christmas Story	34

SECTION II
UNSUNG HEROES

Albert J Ewin	37
Ewing E. La Porte	39
Robert Body	41
Charles Sweeney	43
James Taggart	45

SECTION III
EGYPT FIRE DEPARTMENT

Egypt Fire Association	59
Fund Raising Events	51
4th of July Barn Fire	54
Runaway Truck	56
Fireman Down	58
Hose Testing	60
Exempt Club	62
Cleanest Fireman	64

SECTION VI
MY COCA-COLA YEARS

Friendly Competitors	66
Coke Bleacher Club	68
Special Olympics	71
Cinderella Shoes	74
Opening Day at Silver Stadium	76
Hall of Fame Night	78

SECTION V
MORE FROM THE LIFE AND TIMES OF GENE

Jayne Kennedy	83
Unforgettable Halloween	84
Modern Day Robin Hood	86
Challenges	88
Fire Alarm Wedding	90
The Grandchildren	92
9/11 a Painful Day	95
Tickets for Two	97
My In-Laws	100
On Being a Gentleman	103
A Trip to the Corner Store	105
Transporting Veterans	106
A Street of Veterans	108
McDonald's Award	111

EUGENE SWEENEY

AS I REMEMBER

SECTION I

THE MILITARY LIFE

Corporal Sweeney   Fall 1949

WORLD WAR II SCRAP DRIVE

I grew up on Monroe Parkway in the town of Brighton, just east of Rochester, New York. During the war years from 1941 – 1945 nineteen boys from our street assisted their families by collecting scrap metal. Tin, aluminum cans and any metal we could find was piled in the vacant lot three doors down from my house.

Periodically, the town would send a dump truck to carry the pile to the junk yard.

In those days families also saved newspapers and magazines to earn money to buy school supplies and treats.

Today, junk yards have been replaced by recycling centers. Most towns and cities have bins, that residents use, and their recycle materials are picked up weekly.

How times have changed.

Monroe Parkway Victory Parade of Scrap Metal

These Monroe Parkway, Brighton, youths refer to themselves as the Junior Salvage Army and collect neighborhood scrap to be ready with a mountainous pile when the scrap truck gets there Saturday to take it off to war. They are (left to right) Donald Owens, Tommy Berman, Billy Wiley, Bobby Berman, Gerry Mason, Buddy Hecker, Howard Clark, Johnny Owens and Gaylord Paddock, who carries a gun he is sending along to help defeat the Axis powers. (Times-Union Photo)

They Stand on a 'Bunker Hill of Scrap'

Out in the Monroe Parkway area, Brighton, the junior salvage army rallies. In this hard-working group, left to right on ground, are Phil Sweeney, Kay Wilson, Jack Fitzgerald, Donald Hart; and, atop pile, George Sweeney, Gene Sweeney, Ronald Shacter. They gathered all the scrap they could find and are out again today looking for more.

PEARL HARBOR

On Sunday morning, December 7, 1941, at 7:48 a.m. Hawaiian time, airplanes from the Empire of Japan bombed Pearl Harbor, Hawaii, a U.S. possession. Hawaii had not yet been granted statehood. With the time difference we did not hear about the attack until later that afternoon.

Our family had been out for a ride in our 1937 Ford which had no radio. There were no televisions sets then. We stopped by my Uncle Wendell Toomey's gas station in East Bloomfield, New York. He had his radio playing and the announcers were interrupting the broadcasts to report on the attack.

Many people were unaware of where Pearl Harbor was located. I was 11 years old and my father, a former marine, told me Pearl Harbor was in Hawaii. I was very proud that my Dad knew that.

This attack led our country into World War II, which didn't end until August of 1945.

LOOK BACK AT D-DAY

During World War II, Allied Forces landed on the beaches in Normandy, France on June 6, 1944, D-Day.

United States and British Air Forces had been bombing targets in Europe that were occupied by the Germans.

Earlier, Allied troops had occupied Sicily and made their invasion into Italy, at Anzio. There had not yet been an invasion of ground troops into other parts of Europe that were occupied by Germans.

I was in the eighth grade at the time and remember the principal allowing the news to be heard over the public address system so that all the students and teachers could listen.

We were very concerned for the many former students and teachers who were serving in the Armed Forces at the time.

WORKING DURING WORLD WAR II

Many men and women joined the Armed Forces during World War II, creating a shortage of workers in our country. The government lowered the minimum age for employment from 16 to 14 to ease the problem.

A neighbor on my street, Larry Mooney, was the manager of the Wegmans Food Markets, a family-owned chain in Rochester, New York. Larry promised to hire me when I turned 14. At the time the minimum wage was 37 ½ cents per hour. If I worked a 40 hour week I could make $15, less Social Security withholding tax of one percent.

My first position was working Saturdays bagging groceries at the cashier's counter. On occasion, I assisted the customers by carrying purchases to their cars in the parking lot. Sometimes, if I was lucky, a tip of ten cents to a quarter would be placed in my hand.

Charlie Murray, a friend of my mother, was the grocery manager. He arranged, through Mr. Mooney, to have me work after school stocking shelves. Once school was out in June, I reported daily to the store for work.

Every day we collected returnable soda and beer bottles from customers. After busy weekends there were many bottles to be sorted, placed back into cases and returned to the distributors.

Girls, around my age, worked part-time at the store. Three of the girls, Edna Francis, Betty Cufari and Janet Frohm lived in the town of Pittsford, about five miles away. Edna and I became friendly and I would ride the bus to Pittsford for visits on the weekends. On a couple of occasions, I missed the last bus and had to walk the five miles home. With gas rationing in effect during these times there was little or no traffic on the road to hitch a ride.

About a year later, Louie Angelo, Manager of the Produce Department and his assistant Nick Cocking, asked Mr. Mooney, "Could Gene be transferred from grocery to produce?"

He approved and I was transferred immediately. After school I bagged potatoes from bushel bags into smaller paper bags. Weekends I worked the floor filling fruit bins and waiting on customers. During these times there were no pre-packaged items like we have today. We had to place produce items into bags, then weigh and price them for the customer.

One Saturday the manager and his assistant were gone for the day. They asked if I could take over the department in their absence and call in the orders for fruit and vegetables to be delivered the following Monday. I felt I had been there long enough and could handle the job. My assistants were young boys, like myself. I asked them to come in on Saturday wearing white dress shirts and bow ties. They did as I instructed and later in the afternoon a supervisor from the main office visited the store. He was really impressed with the dress of the boys in the produce department, and from that day forward all employees, male and female, wore black bow ties with white dress shirts.

During this time there were shortages of many staple items such as meat, mayonnaise, tuna fish, coffee and sugar to name a few. As an employee, one of the perks was being there when the delivery of these items arrived at the store. I was able to have them charged to my account and take them home.

After working four years at Wegmans, I graduated high school and went on to other employment. I checked my Social Security record of earnings from 1944 to 1950. My gross income for those six years was $5,591.90, an average of $932.48 per year.

VE DAY

VICTORY IN EUROPE
MAY 8, 1945

The war in Europe ended May 8, 1945. This was called "VE Day," victory in Europe.

The Italian Army who sided with the German Army during the war had surrendered. The Italian Dictator, Benito Mussolini, was dead and Adolf Hitler, the German dictator, committed suicide. The Germans, along with the Axis Powers, agreed to terms of surrender when the Russian Army and the Allied Forces of Great Britain, Canada, France and the United States of America converged on Berlin, Germany from all sides.

Allied troops, who had been engaged on the European front since the "D" day invasion on June 6, 1944, were elated with the news of surrender. The winter of 1944-45 had been severe with rain, snow and cold. Service personnel serving overseas for this duration were sent home to reunite with their families. Younger troops, who had not yet seen action, were re-assigned to the South Pacific Theater in preparation for the invasion of Japan.

AS I REMEMBER

V-J DAY

Victory Over Japan
September 2, 1945

Our armed forces in the South Pacific invaded and captured many islands occupied by the Japanese. Every island brought us a step closer to the mainland of Japan. The death toll, on both sides, was very costly. The mortality rate to military and civilians during the invasion of the Japanese mainland would also be excessive.

The United States had been working on a special project called The Manhattan Project. Engineers and scientists were designing a devastating bomb. One of the biggest decisions of World War II was placed on President Truman when he ordered the atomic bomb dropped on Japan prior to the military invasion of the mainland.

On August 6, 1945, Colonel Paul Tibbets of the Army Air Corps flew his aircraft, the Enola Gay, over the city of Hiroshima, Japan, (a military installation) where the first bomb, called Little Boy, was dropped. The city of Hiroshima was completely annihilated.

When the Japanese government did not surrender after this bomb was dropped, a second bomb, called Fat Man, was dropped on the city of Nagasaki, Japan. The pilot of this aircraft was Major

Charles Sweeney, another Army Air Corps officer from Massachusetts.

Emperor Hirohito then met with his aids and the Empire of Japan accepted the terms of surrender. World War II ended September 2, 1945 when formal papers were signed on the battleship, USS Missouri in Tokyo Bay. This is referred to as "V-J Day" victory over Japan.

I had just turned 15. My Uncle Toot took me downtown, on the local subway, for the celebration. By the time we arrived Main Street was closed to vehicular traffic. People were all over the place, in the streets, in bars and taverns, hugging, kissing, dancing, and waving flags. It was just one BIG celebration I will never forget!

I came home alone on the subway, as I was not of drinking age. My uncle, however, stayed a while longer joining in the crowds excitement and tipping a few.

USMCR

October 16, 1947 – September 1959

In 1935 when I was five years old, I found my dad's Marine uniforms hanging in our attic. That's when I started playing Marine. Four years later I grew into his field uniform.

Gene and his Grandma Sweeney

In 1940 Major E. Frank Doyle, a personal friend of my father, was the Commanding Officer of the Rochester Marine Reserve Unit. His unit was activated for Federal Service that year. They went on to serve in many battles in the Pacific during World War II.

After the war ended in 1945, retired Lieutenant Colonel Doyle assisted in forming another Marine Corps Reserve Company in Rochester. The new unit, "B" Company, 19th Infantry Battalion, was formed in the fall of 1947.

Colonel Doyle had a son, Donald, who was my age. He was the first enlisted man sworn into the Company by his father.

I was asked if I would be interested in joining. My father and I discussed the possibilities. He had served in the Marine Corps during World War I. Dad worked with Frank Doyle at the Rochester Post Office and served with him in the Marine Reserves during the late 1920's.

In September of 1947 I entered my senior year at Brighton High School. In October of 1947 I joined the United States Marine Corp Reserve at age 17, with my parents' consent.

Since World War II was over we felt the chances of another war, in the near future, were slim. As a reservist I would receive pay for attending weekly drills and summer camp.

Drills were held at the East Main Street Armory on Thursday evenings from 7:30 – 9:30 every week.

In June of 1948 I was employed at a local bank and was excused from summer camp. In the Summer of 1949 our Reserve Unit was sent to Camp Lejuene, North Carolina for extensive training.

PRINCE CHARLES

It was Sunday, November 14, 1948. My U.S. Marine Corps Reserve unit in Rochester, New York was invited to participate in the half-time festivities during the pro football game in Buffalo. The ceremonies celebrated the birthday of the Marine Corps on November 10, and Armistice Day on November 11, now called Veterans Day.

After the game, four of us, still in uniform, drove to Niagara Falls for dinner atop the Brock Hotel, overlooking the falls. While we were eating, bells began to ring, music played and spot lights illuminated the falls and scanned the skies in celebration of the birth of Princess Elizabeth's first child Charles, the future Prince of Wales. We toasted the birth of her son. It was a privilege to be in Canada to celebrate this Royal event.

Prince Charles is presently the heir to the British throne. He will become king when his mother, Queen Elizabeth II, abdicates, retires or dies. In Britain the crown normally passes from monarch to eldest son. As King George VI had no son, it passed to his elder daughter, now Queen Elizabeth II.

In 1981, Prince Charles married Dianna Spencer and together they had two children, William and Henry, better known as Harry. Prince Charles and Dianna divorced in 1996.

On April 24, 2011 Prince William married Kate Middleton in the Westminster Cathedral in London. Upon the abdication or death of his father, Prince Charles, Prince William could be heir to the throne.

In 1950 my reserve unit was activated for service during the Korean War. I was assigned to the 6th Marine Regiment of the 2nd Marine Division of Camp Lejeune. My Commanding Officer was first Lieutenant Warren P. DeLand. I became the Clerk of the company. That fall his family joined him in North Carolina. One day while in the office he turned to me and asked, "Sweeney, have you ever been a babysitter?"

I replied, "Yes Sir, I was one of the best babysitters in the town of Brighton."

He asked, "Do you think you're too old to babysit now?"

"No Sir." I replied.

He then picked up the phone to call his wife Sally and informed her they were going to the Officers' Club that evening. That was my first babysitting job while in the service. I enjoyed their daughter Deborah, who was two, and her brother Michael, a few years older. I continued to babysit for them even after I was released from active duty.

I learned the little girl was born on the same day as Prince Charles. She told me in later years her Uncle George did call her Princess. I realized, after all these years, I had been babysitting a Princess!

MARCHING OFF TO WAR

In June of 1950, the North Korean Army, supported by Chinese forces, invaded South Korea, by crossing over the 38th Parallel. (The dividing line between North and South Korea.)

My Reserve Unit was scheduled for summer camp at Little Creek, Virginia for amphibious training exercises the last two weeks of July. While in training we were informed all Marine Reserve Units in the United States were being activated for duty by order of President Harry S. Truman.

On August 19, 1950 our reserve unit was led by my Commanding Officer, Captain Thomas P. Manion from the East Main Street Armory to the Lehigh Valley Railroad Station. Here we assembled on the platform and boarded a troop train for the overnight ride to Camp Lejeune.

While passing through downtown Rochester there was a former marine standing on the curb. He yelled out, "Give 'em hell marines. I was one of you in 1918."

Many family members, neighbors and friends were there to see us off.

My four year enlistment would have been completed in October of 1951; however, all personnel on active duty were extended. My release from the Marine Corps came in May of 1952.

It was then I decided to stay a while longer in the Reserves since I had reached the rank of Staff Sargent. The pay was better and I enjoyed the position. I continued to make summer camps for the next three years.

In January of 1956 I was employed by the Fountain Sales Department of The Coca-Cola Company. My first assignment was Poughkeepsie, New York. While there I became a member of a Marine Volunteer Training Unit (VTU). I was the only enlisted man in the unit.

In 1958 I was transferred to Albany, New York where my work conditions and traveling made it impossible to attend weekly drills. The weekend drill program had not yet been established. I was then transferred to the inactive reserve. Marine Reserve Headquarters, in New York City, notified me that I had met my military obligation and was Honorably Discharged in 1959 having served twelve years in the United States Marine Corps Reserve.

HARDEST THING

While standing in formation on the platform, about to board the troop train for Camp Lejeune, Edward Reifsteck, Athletic Director of my former high school, approached me. Unbeknownst to me, his son Thomas J. Reifsteck, had recently enlisted in our reserve unit. Tom was to start his senior year in high school that September. His father asked me to watch over his son as this was his first time alone and away from home.

Because Tom had not completed high school he would be allowed to return home and graduate with his senior class in June of 1951. After graduation he reported to Parris Island, South Carolina for boot camp and to Camp Lejeune where he received advanced military training. Upon completion of his training he was sent as a replacement to Korea.

Thomas E. Reifsteck was killed in Korea shortly after his arrival. Two other members of our reserve unit (Sergeant Charles Langtree and Corporal Robert Raspanti) were also killed while serving in Korea.

One of the hardest things I ever did was return to my high school to extend my condolences to Tom's father on the loss of his son.

In April of 1986, shortly after our 35th reunion, the former officers and men from "B" Company, 19th Infantry Battalion, USMCR dedicated a bronze memorial plaque with the names of our deceased members to the U.S. Marine Corps Training Center in Rochester, New York.

THE MED CRUISE

After World War II, NATO provided military protection for the countries in the Mediterranean. The 6th Fleet of the U.S. Navy was assigned this duty, with assistance from the United States Marine Corps. My unit, the 6th Marine Regiment 2nd Marine Division, was assigned to this duty in the fall of 1951 for a six month tour of duty on board the USS Latimer.

While on duty, our home port was Naples, Italy. We were in and out of Naples five times between September 1, 1951 and February 1, 1952. Thanksgiving was spent in Greece and the Christmas Holidays in Naples.

When in port, all Sergeants went on Military Police duty with the Navy Shore Patrol every third day. I was on Shore Patrol one day, Liberty one day, and Stand-by Duty one day.

In addition to our protection duty we also put on amphibious landing and training demonstrations for the Italian and Greek armies on Sicily, Sardinia and Crete. Soldiers from Italy and Greece were furnished daily wine allowances. In the evening, around camp fires, we exchanged cigarettes for wine.

Liberty ports included Oran, North Africa, Nice, France, Naples, Italy, Athens, Greece, Valencia, Malta, and Syracusa, Sicily.

Other places visited were Monte Carlo, Monoco, Pompei, Italy and Rome.

During our return trip I took my test for Staff Sergeant. We arrived in the states in Mid-January of 1952 and I was informed I had passed my test and was promoted on March 1. I became the Clerk for the battalion legal officer, Lt. John Lindsay. I was released from active duty on May 30, 1952. I returned to Rochester, New York and joined the 3rd Signal Company USMCR till September 1952.

NICE, FRANCE

While Sergeant Costanza and I were on Shore Patrol Duty in Nice, France we were approached by a girl tightly clutching her coat.

She yelled, "MP, MP, come quick!"

As we approached she opened her coat and we saw she was naked underneath. She told us she had been with a U.S. sailor who had stolen her clothes.

We spotted him on the street, carrying her bra, panties and dress under his arm heading back to the ship. Probably to show his shipmates he had made a score while on liberty in France.

We apprehended the sailor and held him until the Shore Patrol arrived. We then returned the clothing to the young lady.

SERGEANT OF GUARD DUTY

All buck Sergeants had to pull their share of guard duty while aboard ship. We had men on three shifts for four hours each, and then they were relieved. The Officer of the Day made rounds of all posts on every shift.

On the evening of November 31, 1951, Lieutenant Krider asked me to wake him up during the night to make his rounds. He opted to check post alone, but returned and asked me to accompany him to the brig. My sentry on duty was asleep at his post.

The "OD" went up to the sentry and removed his helmet liner causing his head to hit the bulkhead, awakening him with a startled look. Lt. Kriden told me to replace the sentry with a supernumary.

The following morning PFC Trask was called up for Office Hours and demoted in rank for being asleep on post.

ACCIDENTAL SHOOTING

While on liberty in Italy, some Marines purchased small caliber hand guns which were popular in European countries. They were placed in their sea bags for use when they returned to the states for target shooting.

Marine Barney, from our company, was demonstrating his newly acquired pistol when it accidently discharged while aboard ship. The bullet passed between Barney's fingers and struck Marine McClelland in the arm.

A ship's inspection followed the incident. Some weapons were thrown overboard while others were hidden in fire hoses and extra life preservers stored in the lower decks.

Barney was called up for Office Hours and demoted in rank for the incident which injured a fellow Marine.

CHRISTMAS STORY

During the Korean War I served with the 1st Battalion, 6th Marine Regiment. Our unit was part of the 2nd Marine Division and on September 1, 1951 we were militarily transported from Camp Lejeune to Morehead City, North Carolina. Here we boarded U.S. Navy ships for a six month tour of duty in the Mediterranean.

We were anchored in Naples, Italy for Christmas. I celebrated by going to mid-night Mass on Christmas Eve aboard the aircraft carrier USS Roosevelt. All aircraft had been relocated to the flight deck. Troops were transported from their ships in the harbor to the carrier where Mass was conducted on the hangar deck. This deck is directly below the flight deck so everyone was protected from the elements. In Italy, at this time of year, there is a considerable amount of rain.

I returned to my ship, the USS Latimer, about 3 a.m. Christmas Day. The Navy cooks and bakers were busy preparing for the holiday meal. It was customary for Navy Staff to entertain orphan and needy children on festive occasions when in port.

Three children were brought aboard ship on Christmas Day with chaperons. As guests of the U.S. Navy they were fed before the troops. The children were unaccustomed to the American holiday dinner of turkey, stuffing, mashed potatoes, vegetables, rolls and dessert. Much of the food was left untouched. When the military were served their holiday meal, the galley had run out of turkey and substituted ham.

I had the opportunity to meet one of the chaperons who was so grateful the ship's crew had invited the children for Christmas dinner. She gave me her address in Naples and invited me to her home to meet family and relatives.

The following day, while on liberty with two other Marines, we visited at her home. It was a tenement style building with no central heat. The only source of heat was from the kitchen hearth where they did their cooking. Straw mats were placed on the floor for sleeping. Furniture items were very scarce as they were not wealthy. Her family was most gracious and invited us to stay for a pasta dinner.

This Christmas made me realize how fortunate we are to be citizens of our great country and live in the good old USA.

SECTION II

UNSUNG HEROES

Over the last 60 years, during my time in the military and various veterans' organizations, I have met many veterans whom I would refer to as "Unsung Heroes." Five men instantly come to mind. The following short stories are dedicated to their families.

ALBERT J. EWIN

During World War II Al Ewin served in the United States Army in the South Pacific Theatre. His outfit helped liberate the Philippine Islands from the Japanese. He was wounded while serving there and received the Purple Heart.

After the war he enlisted in the Marine Corps Reserve in Rochester, New York. This is where I met Al Ewin. We served together in this outfit.

Our Rifle Company was activated for duty in August of 1950 for service in the Korean War. We were both assigned to "B" Company, 1st Battalion, 6th Marine Regiment at Camp Legeune. This was the home base of the 2nd Marine Division.

Al was given permission to have his automobile on base. This was the vehicle we used to visit our hometown over Thanksgiving and Christmas leaves.

After training from August to December of 1950, Ewin was sent in a replacement draft to Korea with many other Marines. While in Korea he was a member of the 1st Marine Division fighting in the cold weather conditions. He received the Bronze Star for rescuing a wounded comrade and bringing him to safety. Ewin was wounded during the rescue and received his second Purple Heart.

He served in both World War II and Korea. Albert J. Ewin was one of the most highly decorated veterans in our community.

To me he is one of my "Unsung Heroes."

EWING E. LA PORTE

"JOHN"

During the late 1990's, my wife, Lorraine, and I attended the annual Birthday Party for the 2nd Marine Division at Camp Lejeune. At the evening banquet we were seated at a table for eight. One of the men at our table was former Marine John La Porte.

After dinner, Chuck Van Horne, the Executive Director of the Association, announced he had some special guests to introduce. One was a survivor of Wake Island in the South Pacific during World War II.

La Porte was sitting next to me and I heard him say, "I wonder if he's talking about me?"

As a matter of fact he was.

John La Porte entered the Marine Corps in 1940 at the age of 16. Times were difficult in North Carolina at the time and he lied about his age to join. After boot camp he was assigned to Wake Island in the South Pacific Ocean. This outpost was under command of Major James Deveroux. It was here La Porte celebrated his 17th birthday.

In December of 1941 the Japanese bombed Pearl Harbor in Hawaii. Meanwhile the Japanese Army troops started the invasion and occupation of many islands in the South Pacific.

When Wake Island was invaded the small detachment put up a short fight. Those not killed in the battle were being lined up to be shot when a Japanese Naval Officer came ashore and said, "No, we take prisoners."

Survivors were taken by ship to Japan. La Porte was later sent to Occupied China where he spent the duration of the war working in a coal mine.

After serving almost four years as a Prisoner of War, he was repatriated in 1945. He continued his career in the Marine Corps until he retired.

I consider this Marine to be an "Unsung Hero."

ROBERT BODY
"BOB"

Robert Body enlisted in the Canadian Army, unbeknownst to his family, at 16. Needless to say he lied about his age. When his father learned of his whereabouts he interceded and made arrangements for his release.

When Bob turned 17 he went across the border from Windsor, Ontario and entered the United States at Detroit. Here he enlisted in the United States Army. After Basic Training he was assigned to a base in the Philippine Islands in the South Pacific prior to World War II.

In December of 1941 the Japanese Army invaded the Philippines and occupied that country. All American servicemen were taken prisoner by the Japanese. Those still alive made the famous "Bataan Death March." All servicemen were forced to march to their confinement facility. Many died along the way of starvation and lack of water. Those who fell by the wayside were either bayoneted or shot by the Japanese. Body survived the death march and was repatriated in 1945 when the Japanese surrendered.

I met Bob Body after I joined the Morningside Writer Group in Port St. Lucie, Florida. He wrote a book on his experiences on the

"Death March" and his confinement as a Prisoner of War during World War II.

CHARLES W. SWEENEY ATOMIC BOMB PILOT

For those old enough to remember, near the end of World War II, President Harry S. Truman ordered an Atomic Bomb to be dropped on the Japanese homeland. A B-29 bomber, The Anola Gay, flown by an Army Air Corp pilot, Paul Tibbits, dropped the first bomb on Hiroshima, Japan on August 6, 1945.

Military experts thought this devastating bomb would cause the Japanese Empire to surrender immediately. This did not happen and a second bomb was dropped three days later on Nagasaki, Japan which forced the surrender of the Japanese.

The pilot, crew and name of the aircraft dropping the first Atomic Bomb on Hiroshima received much media attention. Not much was heard about the pilot and crew dropping the bomb on Nagasaki.

In the fall of 1997, my wife, Lorraine, and I attended the Annual Meeting of the 2nd Marine Division Association in Boston, Massachusetts. The invited dinner guest was retired Air Force Brigadier General Charles W. Sweeney. The pilot of the B-29 who dropped the second Atomic Bomb on Nagasaki was a native of Massachusetts.

After dinner Lorraine and I introduced ourselves to the General and his wife. I asked, "General, what part of Ireland did your grandfather come from?"

He replied, "County Cork."

I said, "That was the same county my grandfather hailed from. General, we must be distant cousins."

Sweeney's crew also played a role in the bombing of Hiroshima. They flew an instrument plane that accompanied the Enola Gay during the attack. Unfortunately, his crew never got the media attention the first crew received.

In my opinion General Sweeney and his crew were "Unsung Heroes" who helped put the final touches to the end of World War II.

STAFF SERGEANT JAMES TAGGART

During World War II, James Taggart served in the United States Marine Corps. Upon his return, after the war, he became a member of the Boston, Massachusetts Reserve Company. All Marine Reserve units were activated to duty during the Korean War in 1950.

Staff Sergeant Taggart was assigned to "B" Company, 1st Battalion, 6th Marine Regiment of the 2nd Marine Division. This unit was stationed and trained at Camp Lejeune.

On the morning of June 20, 1951 the battalion had been overnight in the field, preparing for a live fire exercise with 81 millimeter mortars. The Mortar section, a part of Weapons Company, was dug in behind my Baker Company. Able and Charlie Companies were out front with my company held in reserve. The exercise was scheduled to commence at 9:00 a.m. (0900 hours military time.) Fog had settled in overnight placing a hold on the exercise until the weather cleared. The sun did not break through until almost noon. We ate lunch and started the training exercise about 1300 hours.

Our Battalion Commander, Lt. Colonel Spurlock, invited Warren De Land, my Company Commander, to join him at the

Command Post. Executive Officer, Nicolas Aguzin, was in charge. When the exercise began Able and Charlie Companies were advancing to their primary position. Mortars commenced their overhead barrage of fire toward the secondary target. After the primary position was secured our unit was to move up and relieve one of the forward companies.

That day I was the radio operator for our company. Shortly after the mortars fired their first salvo I heard screaming calls coming in over my radio.

"Cease fire, cease fire, rounds landing short, men injured!"

Rounds from the mortars accidently landed short, exploding on trees overhead spreading shrapnel over the troops on the ground.

Staff Sergeant James Taggart, veteran of World War II, overheard the radio communication. He immediately contacted Lt. Aguzin requesting he take our corpsmen to the scene as they would be needed there. Permission was granted.

General Clifton B. Cates, Commandant of the Marine Corps was visiting Camp Lejeune that day. He immediately ordered a Board of Inquiry. Later it was determined two faulty mortar rounds had landed short, exploding when hitting the treetops in this heavily wooded area. Shrapnel from the blast killed eight Marines. Twenty-three were wounded, one critically, eight seriously. The highest ranking enlisted man killed was Able Company's First Sergeant C. P. Czerviec from Philadelphia, Pennsylvania.

It was a sad day for all who participated.

In my opinion, Staff Sergeant Taggart is an "Unsung Hero." Having the presence of mind and quick thinking to assist injured Marines on this training exercise he should have been considered for, and awarded, a Medal for Heroism.

EUGENE SWEENEY

SECTION III
EGYPT
FIRE
DEPARTMENT

EGYPT FIRE ASSOCIATION

The Egypt Fire Association is a volunteer fire department located three miles east of Fairport, New York in the hamlet of Egypt. Not the Egypt in North Africa, where they have blowing and drifting sand, but we were often referred to as "The Camel Drivers." Egypt, New York is the eastern most community of Monroe County, situated on state route 31, the old post road, connecting Rochester with towns and cities to the east.

Stagecoaches ran through this hamlet in the early days and there were two inns where travelers spent the night. They were the Staples Inn and the McGraw's Inn. This rural community consisted mainly of farmers and in 1946 the residents decided it was time to establish a Fire Protection District to protect dwellings and property in the area.

The Egypt Fire Association was formed with the purchase of a used fire truck from the Sampson Naval Training Station, formerly a boot camp for the United States Navy during World War II.

I joined the department in 1965 after I purchased my home within the fire district. At that time the department had four vehicles;

an emergency truck, a tank truck, an International pumper truck and the original truck, which had become a grass fire truck.

FUND RAISING EVENTS

After a volunteer fire department is established many communities find adequate funds are not always available to support financing. These departments conduct fund raising activities during the year. Our department held ham dinners, turkey raffles, sold steamed clams, and ran bingo games in addition to our annual fund drive. The ladies auxiliary assisted us by selling recipe books, holding craft sales and auctions.

The annual fund drive contributed greatly to our source of revenue. In addition, every year members went house to house, knocking on doors and ringing the bells of local residents asking, or more accurately, begging for funds. Our department had no uniforms, except for the navy blue, bell shaped fireman's hat, which members purchased. The department furnished a Maltase cross shaped fireman's badge to adorn the hat.

My first year of participation in the fund drive was in 1966. I went to one house where an Afro-American lady answered the door. She was dressed in a white uniform and I thought she was a nurse caring for a sick resident or a maid cleaning the house. I noticed she went to a pocketbook, bringing a cash donation. My summation was that the resident of this house trusted this lady highly.

I reported back to the fire truck and relayed my experience to the other firemen who began to laugh. They informed me that house was owned by an Afro-American family. Both husband and wife were licensed pharmacists who owned a pharmacy in Rochester, New York.

I later became acquainted with her husband who eventually joined our department. He resigned after serving about one year. Much later he confided to me that during a drill he had slipped and fallen off the back of the truck, broke his wrist, and was too embarrassed to report it.

The most enjoyable fund raisers were during the summer months when we sold steamed clams. We assisted neighboring departments at their carnivals too, selling our steamed clams in bags of one dozen. Cleaning and bagging the clams was hard work. Clams were just one of the food delicacies at these carnivals.

Each year we conducted our "Turkey Raffle" at the fire hall, prior to Thanksgiving. We moved all the trucks outside to make room for residents and neighboring firemen converging on the Egypt Fire Department. Chairs were placed on the truck room floor where fire personnel sold, and visitors purchased, raffle tickets. After the wheel turned round and round, the winner of that spin received a ten to twelve pound frozen turkey.

To keep visitors in attendance during the evening the department furnished free draft beer, soft drinks and homemade sandwiches for all. Many visitors roasted their prize turkeys on

Thanksgiving Day. Next to the Annual Awards Banquet the Turkey Raffle was the big social event of the year.

4th OF JULY BARN FIRE

Every year residents in my neighborhood of Rolling Hill, Matthew Drive and Starlight Circle in Fairport, New York gathered at someone's home to celebrate the fair weather holidays of Memorial Day, Fourth of July and Labor Day. My wife and I hosted the 1966 Fourth of July outing.

Neighbors played croquet and tossed jarts. (A lawn game where you throw a pointed projectile, with fins, underhanded to a circular target placed on the grass in the yard.) The quarter keg of beer was on ice in the garage and the grill, in the driveway, was cooking hot dogs when the fire siren from the Egypt Fire Department sounded in mid-afternoon. The dispatcher announced over the radio that the barn on Frankie Gerber's property, a brother fireman, was burning. We looked east, from my front yard scenic view, and observed the smoke rising from the barn.

I turned my chef's responsibilities of grilling hot dogs over to a neighbor. Another volunteer fireman, Bill McGeary, and I left by car and went to the fire station, where we hopped aboard a fire truck and went directly to the scene. The barn was filled with hay in the loft and it was "going good," meaning it was burning fast and out of control. We knew the barn could not be saved so we poured water on the house and other out buildings to save them.

Upon my return home I found the guests had eaten their hots and drank their fill of cold beer, while watching the barn burn from the excellent view in my front yard, approximately two miles away.

The department kept an all-night vigil to insure no embers would re-kindle during the night and start another fire. I volunteered for an early morning assignment from one to three a.m. Frankie broke out his favorite homemade hard apple cider for those who joined him on that all-night vigil.

What an end to the Fourth of July.

RUNAWAY TRUCK

EARLY 1970'S

Sunday morning was the time for truck maintenance at the fire hall. I was not scheduled for duty this particular Sunday. As I was on my way to fill the gas tank on our car I drove by the hall and pulled in to talk with the boys who were outside, with boots on, washing the truck.

While we chatted in front of the building the fire siren whaled. The dispatcher reported a shed fire, behind a residence, on Route 31.

The boys said, "You drive, you don't have boots on."

I jumped out of my car and hopped aboard Engine P-14, the International pumper. The men in boots boarded the back of the truck. Fortunately, there was a fire hydrant nearby the house. I stopped at the hydrant, and the men in the rear pulled off the hose and connected it to the fire plug.

I drove the truck up the inclined driveway, leaving behind a snake-like coil of two and one half inch hose. The shed was at the rear of the house and I stopped the truck close to the shed, set the micro-lock brakes and engaged the pump. Our truck was the first on the scene and we had the fire out by the time the other trucks arrived.

After the blaze was extinguished, I shut down the pump. Shortly thereafter my truck started to roll backwards. By instinct I dove into the open door of the cab and re-set the emergency brake. The truck rolled back a few more inches where the rear dual tires were halted by a crooked fire hose, charged with water, we dragged behind us.

We were lucky. I knew our new Ford pumper truck had parked right behind me for backup. Had the charged hose not been there, my truck would have rolled backwards, down the inclined driveway, and into our new truck. This could have been a costly and embarrassing problem for the department.

The older truck I was driving did not have air brakes. They were hydraulic brakes and a brake line had broken allowing fluid to escape making the brakes inoperable.

On my dive into the cab to re-set the emergency brake, I tore muscles and ligaments in my chest. I lived with a sore chest while my body healed.

Just one of many memorable experiences while serving as a volunteer fireman.

FIREMAN DOWN

It was after mid-night, with the temperatures below zero. That's cold! A call came in over my fire radio reporting a house fire on the upper hills of Thayer Road in our district. The house was located outside the hydrant area and our chief immediately requested services for Mutual Aid from neighboring fire departments asking them to send tank trucks to haul needed water to the scene.

Upon arriving at the house, Ray Wolfe and I entered the building from the rear porch to attack the fire, while another team entered from the front. Ray was the nozzle man and I was behind him assisting with the hose. Emergency lighting had not yet been placed as power to the house had been cut off. From the porch we inched our way into the house when the floor suddenly gave way under Ray and he fell into the cellar below. I grabbed the hose nozzle, which he had dropped, and shut off the flow of water.

On instinct I stopped. In the dark of night I did not want to fall through the same hole and land on top of Ray. I called down, "You okay?"

He replied, "I don't think I'm hurt, just shaken up."

I yelled for assistance and for portable lights to shine into the basement and a ladder. Fortunately, Ray was not injured and was able to climb out of the cellar. We were relieved knowing our brother fireman came out unscathed.

The cause of the fire was an overheated fireplace in a very old farm house on an extremely cold night.

HOSE TESTING

After a fire, flood or disaster effects businesses or damages buildings it is normally the Board of Health, or another government agency, that orders them to be closed or temporarily shut down. In this scenario it was the result of hose testing by the Egypt Volunteer Fire Department.

Every year all fire departments in New York State are required to pressure test the hose they carry on their vehicles. Over time hoses rot from sitting around, or are damaged from wear and tear after having been dragged over pavement.

The Fire Department officers scheduled different men each month for maintenance duty. Every Sunday morning we followed a check-off procedure on all the equipment. Four vehicles carried two and one half inch diameter hose; a grass fire truck, two pumper trucks and the aerial extension ladder truck.

Our chief picked a bright, clear Sunday morning and requested all company members attend the annual hose testing exercise. This was conducted in a new housing development across the street from the Perinton Square Shopping Plaza. New fire hydrants had been installed, and were in working condition, but no one was yet living in the new development. A picture perfect setting for hose testing.

We had almost completed the testing exercise when a Monroe County Sheriff's deputy came by. He informed the chief that the Perkins Restaurant, in the plaza across the highway reported muddy and murky tap water. Customers were complaining about poor tasting coffee.

That Sunday morning Perkins Restaurant was filled with patrons, but had to close its doors due to the water problem. We had been drawing water from the new hydrants stirring up the sediment in the water main, the same line serving Perkins.

Fortunately, our department didn't have to reimburse the restaurant for their loss of revenue.

After this experience, the fire department did their hose testing at more remote locations within our fire district.

Unfortunately, from that day on we had to find another place for our free coffee.

EXEMPT CLUB

John Brackett, a former president of the Egypt Fire Association, was instrumental in forming our Egypt Exempt Club. This group consists of all members completing five years of active service as volunteer fireman. The Exempt Club members are entitled to special privileges; they become exempt from serving jury duty in New York State.

Our Exempt Club held quarterly meetings. Some were dinner meetings, held away from the fire hall, at local restaurants. This particular quarterly meeting was at the Green Lantern Inn, a restaurant in Fairport, New York. That night I drove and picked up my neighbor Bill, also a volunteer fireman.

After the meeting Bill made arrangements for a ride home with another fellow fireman. He wanted to stay longer to chat with other members. I came home alone, parked the car in the garage and went to bed.

Bill's wife, Betty, saw my car pull into the driveway. She noticed her husband not with me. It was now late and she thoughtfully decided not to telephone.

After careful consideration she dressed and drove to the restaurant. Upon arrival she found all the Egypt firemen had departed.

In the meantime Bill returned home. He noticed Betty was not at home and thought nothing of it. It was not unusual for her to visit neighbors, so he just went to bed.

When Betty came home she found Bill, in bed, fast asleep.

Bill awoke the next morning and remarked, "You were out late last night."

CLEANEST FIREMAN

Volunteer Fire Departments are always looking for new members. Interested candidates are interviewed by a screening committee then placed on probation to see how well they adapt.

New volunteers in the Egypt Fire Association are given a fire radio which is activated by the County Fire Dispatcher. This alert from the radio informs all personnel of an existing emergency and its location.

Jason Johnson became a probationary member and was issued his radio. His first emergency call came in during the middle of the night. Most members grab their clothes and respond immediately to the fire hall.

On this night Jason got up from his bed, went to the bathroom, brushed his teeth, took a shower, and dressed in his utility fire department uniform. Then he reported to the fire station.

The call received happened to be a minor one. All the apparatus had returned to the fire hall before Jason arrived.

When asked by an officer, "Why did it take you so long to respond?"

He answered, "I had to get cleaned up."

The chief informed Jason. "If you want to pass your probationary period you will have to respond much faster."

AS I REMEMBER

SECTION IV
MY COCA-COLA YEARS

Gene at Silver Stadium 1982

FRIENDLY COMPETITORS

In 1959 I was transferred by the Coca-Cola Company from Albany, New York back to my home town of Rochester. One night I had to pick up a prescription at the local drug store.

While there the druggist asked me, "Do you know the gentleman standing in the aisle in the front of the store?"

I replied, "No Sir."

He said, "He's your competitor, Frank Starpoli, President of The Rochester Pepsi-Cola Bottling Company."

I walked over and introduced myself.

We exchanged courtesies and Mr. Starpoli said, "If you ever need a job, come see me."

We both resided in the town of Perinton and belonged to the same Catholic Church. The church was in the midst of a fund drive and I was on the committee. No one wanted to call on Frank so I volunteered. One evening I phoned him and he informed me he would be glad to contribute.

On another occasion my boss, Henry Rapsis, was with me. My company car was not air-conditioned and we had the windows down while we were stopped at a red light in downtown. A car pulled alongside of us and the driver, in his air-conditioned vehicle, lowered his window. It was Frank Starpoli. We exchanged cordialities, the light changed and we proceeded on our way.

Henry asked, "Who was that?"

I told him, "The President of the Rochester Pepsi-Cola Bottling Company."

He shook his head, not realizing we knew one another.

While working for Coca-Cola we had to submit bids to many organizations. Local Canada Dry, Coca-Cola and Pepsi distributors submitted their company's proposals. I had the opportunity to meet all of my competitors at various events. We always exchanged friendly experiences.

Unfortunately, Mr. Starpoli died very unexpectedly. The President of Coca-Cola Bottling Company, Mr. Len Anderson, knew I was acquainted with Mr. Starpoli and requested we attend the funeral service together.

Mr. Starpoli was a great man and supported many charities in my hometown of Rochester, New York.

COKE BLEACHER CLUB

Rochester, New York had operated a professional baseball team in the International League for many years. In the 1980's the Red Wings were a farm team for the Baltimore Orioles of the American League.

William "Bill" Farrell, Assistant Superintendent of the Rush Henrietta School District, was President of the Rochester Community Baseball Club. The Board of Directors of the ball club was disappointed with the low attendance in the bleacher section, so Mr. Farrell contacted Harvey E. Anderson, the President of the Rochester Coca-Cola Bottling Corporation, to see if his company was interested in leasing the bleachers at Silver Stadium for one year as a promotional venture. Mr. Anderson agreed, and hence the Coke Bleachers Club was created.

As an employee at Rochester Coke, I was appointed Coordinator for the Coke Bleacher Club. Red baseball caps imprinted with, "Coke Bleacher Club" were ordered. These caps were sold for $5.00 each and entitled the wearer of the cap to free admission to all home games in the bleacher section at Silver Stadium. Initially 1,000 caps were ordered. When the media notified the public, the response was overwhelming. Two more orders were placed for a total of 3,000 caps. This entitled a family to sit together in the bleacher section and enjoy all home games.

The old bleachers were made of wood and in disrepair. One Saturday while the team was out of town, all Bleacher Club members were invited to the stadium to sand and paint the bleachers. The old flag pole located at the end of the bleacher section was repainted and restrung with new rope. We had a great turnout and provided hot dogs and Coke for all the volunteers. A large red Coca-Cola flag was placed in the bleacher section and flew at all home games. What a sight to see the red flag and the fans wearing their red Coke Bleacher caps.

The first year's promotion was very successful. The Bleacher Club fans were growing strong and elected "Rusty" May as their president. During that winter the club held its Annual Meeting at Sweet's Party House in Webster, New York. It was here that Rusty was presented with an award for being the first President of the Coke Bleacher Club.

Coke management decided to continue the promotion for the next year. A Bleacher Cap Pin was designed to attach to the red hats and was sold for $5.00 each, allowing free admission to the Coke Bleachers for the second year. Throughout the following years, red Coke "T" Shirts imprinted with "Coke Bleacher Club" were sold for $5.00 each and once again became a member's admission ticket to the Coke Bleachers for another year.

With the popularity of the Coke Bleachers, fans continued to return to the bleacher section at Silver Stadium. Eventually, Red Wing management elected to replace the old wooden bleachers with new aluminum ones.

One day a month, during the home season, Rochester Coca-Cola provided a "Coke Night" in the bleachers, providing free Coca-Cola and hot dogs for all club members in attendance. Members from the club volunteered to cook the hot dogs and dispense the drinks.

In 1986, Rochester Coca-Cola was sold by the Anderson family to a firm from Pennsylvania. Years later, the new management decided not to continue leasing the bleacher section at Silver Stadium and that was the end of the great Coke Bleacher Fan Club.

SPECIAL OLYMPICS

SUMMER 1979

The International Special Olympic Track and Field Games were held at Brockport State Teachers College in Brockport, New York during the summer of 1979. Coco-Cola USA, with its headquarters in Atlanta, Georgia, was one of the sponsors of the three day event.

Over 3,000 contestants were enrolled to compete for their respective countries. With the college closed for the summer, Olympians and their chaperons were housed in the dormitories on campus.

This event was held in the franchise territory of the Rochester Coca-Cola Bottling Company. The President of the franchise, Harvey Anderson, called me into his office informing me of our company's role in the event. My job was to contact all local food merchants in the Brockport area, inviting them to participate on the campus grounds. They were to set up their food stands for the public using Coca-Cola products.

Over 10,000 visitors were expected each day, commencing with the opening ceremony on Friday night up to the closing ceremony on Sunday afternoon. Many celebrities were invited to greet and meet the world class Special Olympians. Among some of the sports personalities were boxing great, Muhammad Ali and one of baseball's super stars Henry (Hank) Aaron of the Atlanta Braves. He stopped by our service tent to have his picture taken with our set up and service crew.

On Friday evening we met the Coca-Cola corporate airplane at the airport and transported their representatives to the Brockport Teachers College for the Opening Ceremonies. For Identification purposes, all our executives and celebrities in attendance wore VIP badges.

When the Olympians saw our badges, they would ask our staff members, "Are you a movie star?"

A special tent was erected on the grounds for the athletes. They came in anytime during the day for free Coca-Cola fountain drinks. Having met with the college officials prior to the event, arrangements were made to have an additional supply of 12 ounce cans stored on campus in the event the dispensing machines malfunctioned. Fortunately, there were no problems with the equipment during the games.

However, on Sunday afternoon I was paged to report to the administration tent. As I entered the tent, I was approached by the college vice-president. He said, "Gene, we forgot about providing soft drinks for the athletes at the dances tonight in the two gymnasiums. Is there anything you can do for us?"

The warehouse with the 12 ounce cans stored on campus was put to use. Volunteers picked up empty metal garbage containers from the dorms and placed large plastic bags into each container and filled them with cans of Coke products. All containers were then cooled with ice from campus good service department and resolved the soft drink dilemma. The athletes not only enjoyed the dance but were refreshed with their fill of delicious and refreshing Coca-Cola products.

My boss, who was in attendance, asked about me being paged, "What was that all about?"

After I gave him my report of the day's events, he was extremely pleased with what I had done. That Monday morning he called me into his office and mentioned how delighted he was with the results and how things were handled in Brockport for the International Special Olympic Games. Other than PGA and LPGA golf tournaments, this was the largest three-day Special Event our company had ever participated in. My reward was an extra weeks pay plus one extra week of paid vacation, making me a very pleased employee.

CINDERELLA SHOES

Part of my duties as Director of Customer Relations for Rochester Coca-Cola Bottling Company was to handle customer complaints. One day I received a phone call from a lady informing me our product had damaged a pair of her shoes. This happened while she was walking by a floor display of Coca-Cola in a local supermarket. A six pack had fallen breaking the bottles and spraying her feet with coke.

She asked, "Would Coca-Cola replace her ruined shoes?"

I said, "We will have to see the shoes first. Once approved you could go to a local shoe store to have the shoes replaced. Then send us the receipt for reimbursement."

She said, "These shoes are a 'specialty item' and have to be ordered from the Cinderella Shop in Boston, Massachusetts."

I met her at her residence to view the damaged shoes. Meanwhile one of our employees confirmed there had been an accident at the store.

Her home, with double front doors approximately eight feet high, was located in the older section of the city. The bottom third of the doors was solid. The upper two thirds was glass, covered with curtains making it difficult to see in. When standing outside you would normally see a shadow of a person coming to answer the door.

I rang the doorbell. I could not see any shadows. However, the door began to open. It was a rather eerie feeling.

Standing inside, hidden by the lower part of the door, was a "little person" (dwarf) in her housecoat. She invited me in and I sat down in a full size chair while she hopped up onto the sofa.

I learned that local shoe stores do not carry adult size shoes in the children's department and the ladies department does not carry extremely small adult shoes. I saw the damaged shoes and instructed her to order a replacement pair from the Cinderella Shop and send us the bill.

Before leaving, I left a complimentary case of Coca-Cola with her.

OPENING DAY AT SILVER STADIUM

In 1985, I was an Account Executive for the Rochester Coco-Cola Bottling Corporation. The local Red Wing Baseball Team played their home games in the International League at Silver Stadium, named for Morrie Silver, a well-known local entrepreneur.

The opening day was held on April 11th and I had purchased a box seat for four people. My guests included a neighbor school teacher, a vice president of a local bank, and the owner of two McDonald's restaurants in the area.

It was a cold 45 degree opening day, with wind gusts up to 25 mph. My guests were warmly dressed in overcoats, gloves and caps. We were so bundled up we caught the eye of Andy Pollock, a sports writer for the local Democrat & Chronicle Newspaper.

Andy came to us and asked, "Do you mind if I interview you?"

I said, "No, not if the others don't object."

They all agreed. My guests in the front box seats, the teacher and the banker were interviewed first.

The restaurant owner said to the reporter, "I am watching my first Opening Day from a seat in the stands rather than a spot on the field."

The reporter asked, "What's your name?"

He replied, "Herb Washington."

The reporter said, "You're kidding, aren't you?"

I said to Herb, "Take your glove off."

He did and there was the gold World Series ring from the 1974 World Champion Oakland A's.

Reporter Pollock replied, "You weren't kidding were you?"

As cold as it was, it was a most enjoyable afternoon of baseball, eating hot dogs and sipping beer.

HALL OF FAME NIGHT

In 1986 the Rochester Red Wing Baseball Club established a Hall of Fame for the Red Wing baseball players at Silver Stadium. I was asked by the General Manager Robert "Bob" Goughn, to serve on the Hall of Fame Selection Committee. I served on this committee for five years prior to my retiring from Rochester Coca-Cola in 1991.

Russ Derry, a former outfielder and great batsman, was selected, with other players, to be the first inductees at the Ceremony at Silver Stadium. I had the opportunity to escort Russ onto the field for the pre-game ceremony, where the inductees were presented with their awards.

After the pre-game festivities I sat with my friends Len and Sylvia Korn in their box seat. While sitting there two young boys recognized me from having been on the field.

They were standing behind the box and Sylvia overheard one say, "He was on the field. Let's ask him for his autograph. It might be worth something someday."

I signed the baseballs and Sylvia kidded me about my famous autograph.

Later, I purchased a Red Wing baseball, autographed it and mailed it to Sylvia with a note, "This ball may be worth something someday."

I retired from the Coca-Cola and received a very special gift.

This is to certify that the flag presented with this certificate was flown over the Capitol of the United States especially for presentation to

W. EUGENE SWEENEY

ON THE OCCASION OF YOUR RETIREMENT FROM COCA-COLA AFTER 35 YEARS OF OUTSTANDING SERVICE AND LOYALTY

DATE FLOWN July 4, 1990

Frank Horton
Member of Congress

AS I REMEMBER

A letter from Senator Ralph Quattrociocci upon my retirement

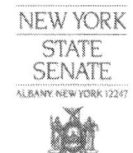

NEW YORK STATE SENATE
ALBANY, NEW YORK 12247

RALPH QUATTROCIOCCHI
SENATOR, 55TH DISTRICT

COMMITTEES
LOCAL GOVERNMENT
RANKING MINORITY MEMBER
AGING
CITIES
FINANCE
TRANSPORTATION
TOURISM, RECREATION AND
SPORTS DEVELOPMENT
VETERANS

DISTRICT OFFICE
1577 RIDGE ROAD WEST
ROCHESTER, NEW YORK 14615
716-663-7200

ALBANY OFFICE
ROOM 615
LEGISLATIVE OFFICE BUILDING
ALBANY, NEW YORK 12247
518-435-3444

June 1, 1991

Eugene Sweeney
c/o Holiday Inn
Genesee Plaza
120 E. Main Street
Rochester, NY 14604

Dear Gene:

I would like to add my name to the long list offering congratulations upon your retirement.

Your work ethic and dedication will be sorely missed at the Coca-Cola Bottling Company. Your public relations efforts helped highlight the generosity of the Rochester Coca-Cola company and its commitment to the community.

At the same time, your involvement with numerous civic and charitable organizations has been widely recognized. It takes a special person to offer their free time to help others. Your abilities have served as a motivational factor for others.

Congratulations. I wish you the best in all your future endeavors.

Sincerely,

Ralph Quattrociocchi
Ralph Quattrociocchi
Senator, 55th District

RQ:cpl

SECTION V
MORE FROM THE LIFE OF AND TIMES OF GENE

JAYNE KENNEDY

In 1983 I was on the Dinner Selection Committee for the Charity Sport Banquet sponsored by the Rochester Press-Radio Club. The dinner committee made arrangements for Jayne Kennedy to be the Honored Guest.

I was asked to make the necessary travel arrangements by contacting Miss Kennedy's agent in California. When contacting her agent I was informed Miss Kennedy always flies "First Class."

I made arrangements with the hotel to use their limousine to pick up Miss Kennedy at the airport. She and I rode in the back seat of the limo from the airport to the hotel. Upon arrival I escorted her to the front desk where she registered.

Needless to say, my fellow club members were a bit envious.

UNFORGETTABLE HALLOWEEN

One fall evening in the early 1980's, my wife, Mary, and I were returning to our home in Fairport, New York.

While driving along Ayrault Road, after dark, the headlights shined on the form of a hitchhiker along the roadside. I spotted the red hair and slowed down.

My wife said, "Why are you stopping?"

"It's our neighbor, the Harris kid from Matthew Drive," I said.

I stopped the car and he jumped in the back seat. He said, "Thanks Mr. Sweeney for picking me up." He was about a mile and a half from his home, still a good walk. On the way he commented, "Boy, all the neighbor kids love to go to your house for Halloween. You give out the biggest and best candy bars."

Upon dropping him off at his house, he said, "Thanks again. See ya."

We never saw the boy again.

In early October while we were vacationing in Florida I telephoned our neighbors, the McGearys. They kept an eye on our house while we were away.

During the conversation, they mentioned a neighbor kid had been killed in an automobile accident at the corner of Ayrault and Aldridge roads, just a short distance from our home.

I asked, "Who?"

"The Harris boy."

We returned home for Halloween. The red-headed Harris boy did not stop for his candy bar that year.

It was a sad Halloween for us.

MODERN DAY ROBIN HOOD

At the end of World War II, the Diocese of Rochester, New York granted permission to our parish pastor to build a new parochial grade school. Parishioners were looking forward to educating their children with a Catholic background.

My brother Phil and I had already graduated from grammar school, however, my youngest brother Leo, was the right age. Our parents decided to send him for some parochial education before he entered high school.

When the new building was completed he entered the fifth grade at Our Lady of Lourdes. The Saint Joseph nuns were the teachers and administrators. Nuns always had a worthy cause to pursue and they instituted a Mission Baby Charity Program for youngsters in foreign countries.

For every five dollars collected a "Mission Baby" would receive food, clothing, shelter and medicine for a given period of time. Nuns also had polite ways of asking for money from the students to assist the needy. All children were asked to donate money for this project. Every week students brought in their donations to support the newly formed charity.

Each year the faculty conducted an open house where parents met with teachers to discuss the progress of the students. My mother always attended, and she was greeted this evening by an ecstatic nun. The nun reported that contributions to the Mission Baby Program, made by Leo were leading all students in the school.

The following morning mother confronted Leo. "I was talking to one of the nuns last night and she said you were the leading contributor to the Mission Baby Program. Imagine my surprise since I didn't even know about the program and didn't contribute. You don't have an after school job. So I was just wondering where you got this money."

Leo was quite proud and announced, "I got it from Uncle Toot"

Mom was skeptical, "He gave you the money?"

Leo explained, "No, not exactly. I got it from the jar in his closet. I'm like Robin Hood, taking from the rich and giving to the poor."

My Mother's brother, Wallace Toomy, lived with us. He enjoyed playing cards and kept his poker winnings in a jar in his bedroom closet.

Needless to say, Leo was reprimanded for his stealing ways. I am sure the "Mission Baby Program" encountered a minor set-back with the loss of funds from Leo and his uncle.

Unfortunately, Uncle Toot was unable to write off this charitable loss on his income tax.

CHALLENGES

Many people have forgotten January 28, 1986.

I have not.

There were three sad incidents this date that I remember vividly.

The Space Shuttle Challenger, with school teacher Christa McAuliffe, took off from Cape Canaveral. The spacecraft did not make a successful launch and all crew members were lost shortly after the launch.

Later that same day I met with the home health care nurse. She made weekly visits to our home to check on my first wife due to her advanced cancer. Mary was unable to walk without assistance. Her oncologist told us to notify him when she could no longer manage at home. It was on this day we called her doctor for advice. He directed us to bring her to the hospital. I called an ambulance while the nurse prepared her for the trip.

After admission I returned home to call my brother-in-law to inform him of his sister's condition. He was not home when I called.

That evening he called to tell me their mother had died that day in Massachusetts. I told him of his sister's re-admission to the hospital.

The following morning our pastor joined me at the hospital to inform Mary of her mother's passing. Mary requested I attend her mother's funeral, 300 miles away. This was one of the hardest decisions of my life. It was her wish and I went. Married for almost 30 years, Mary died 15 days later on February 12, 1986.

FIRE ALARM WEDDING

My bride-to-be, Lorraine La Chance, and I rented a home in Port St. Lucie, Florida for the winter of 1992-1993. While living there we found a new community named St. Lucie Gardens. The community consisted of two bedroom villas on a small lake. We really loved Florida and were looking for a place to live, so we put in an offer, moving into our new home at the end of January 1993.

With our wedding planned for later that year, we left Florida in early May and drove to Fairport, New York where I still owned a home. Invitations were mailed and friends and family from New England and New York came for the event. We were married on May 29th with Mardene Beardsley as her Maid of Honor and daughters, Patti and Renee, as Bridesmaids. My youngest brother Leo was my Best Man.

Our wedding reception was held in the Rochester Suite on the 14th floor of the Holiday Inn, downtown Rochester. That same evening one of the local high schools was having their Senior Prom in the Ballroom downstairs.

About 11 p.m. the fire alarm sounded. The elevators were shut down as was the procedure. All hotel guests were instructed to vacate the building. Our reception guests, with cocktails in hand, walked down 14 flights of stairs.

When the Rochester Fire Department officials sounded the all clear, we rode the elevators back to the reception for more partying.

An hour or so later the alarm sounded again.

Exasperated, Lorraine called the front desk and asked, "Do we really have to evacuate again?"

"Yes. I'm sorry those are the rules."

She turned to her guests and said, "Party on."

A day never to be forgotten.

THE GRANDCHILDREN

At the time of our wedding Renee was expecting her first child. We were very excited as this would be our first grandchild. The day after the wedding, a baby shower was held at our home for the expectant mother, with most of the family members attending.

June 26, 1993, almost a month later, my Brighton High School graduation class held its 45th year reunion. Our banquet was held at the Monroe Country Club in Pittsford, New York. After the festivities of the evening we went to bed quite late.

In the early hours of that morning we were awakened by a telephone call from Jon Mesh, our son-in-law, informing us Renee was in the hospital with labor pains. She wasn't due until September, so this was a troubling call.

Lorraine was very concerned for her daughter and grandchild. We hurriedly packed, jumped into our car and took off for the hospital in Albany, New York, 200 miles away.

Lorraine, upset and crying, prayed that her daughter and the baby would be okay. As we drove across the New York State Thruway toward Albany she suddenly stopped crying. She turned to me and said, "Everything is fine. An Angel just told me she's had the baby and he's fine."

Upon arrival at the hospital (actually it was a Birthing Center) we found Renee sitting up in bed and Christian Andrew Mesh, our new grandson, in an incubator for infants. He was born on June 27, 1993, weighing less than four pounds. Being a three month "premie" he remained in the hospital until he reached five pounds before his parents could bring him home. What a great thrill knowing everything turned out fine.

*   *   *   *

In 1995 we sold our property in Fairport and became permanent residents of Florida. Our stay in "The Gardens" lasted six years. In 1998, we began looking for a three bedroom home since our two bedroom villa was a bit small when company arrived with children. I also needed office space.

We found our present home in the fall of 1998. The house, situated on a lake in the Villages of Lake Lucie, became our dream home. We submitted an offer in October of that year, which was accepted. The owners were building their new home and would not be able to vacate until April of 1999. We placed our home on the market and it sold before we moved.

Moving day was April 17, 1999. Old friends and neighbors assisted with the move. Fortunately, our telephone had already been installed because during the turmoil that day, the phone rang. It was our son-in-law calling from Albany, New York informing us our second grandson, Noah William Mesh, was born that morning. We will never forget our moving day into our new home on Sand Pine Circle in Port St Lucie.

This year, 2006, Christian celebrated his 13th birthday in June and Noah turned seven in April.

We have two wonderful healthy grandchildren, each with an interesting birth story for us to remember.

9/11 A PAINFUL DAY

My wife Lorraine and I were at home the morning of September 11, 2001. She was watching a TV program in the bedroom, while I read the newspaper in the kitchen. She was watching the "Today" show when a special broadcast announced an airplane had crashed into the side of the World Trade Center in New York City.

At first, I thought a small aircraft veered off course or encountered engine failure. I joined her to watch the television report. As we both watched, another large jetliner came into view and crashed into Trade Center Tower II. Now both towers were burning and smoke filled. We were shocked by what we had just witnessed.

We learned later that terrorists had commandeered four commercial airliners loaded with jet fuel and passengers. These aircraft were flown into pre-selected targets in the United States.

People from all floors of the damaged buildings scurried to escape. Burning jet fuel from the ruptured gas tanks created excessive heat causing the superstructures to weaken. Within three hours both towers of the World Trade Center had collapsed to the ground, creating a monster smoke cloud all over the city. More than 3,000 people were trapped inside, most of whom died. Firemen, policemen, workers, and visitors to the building were among the victims.

I was deeply saddened by the events of that day. It will be long remembered as a date in the record books as the worst terrorist tragedy in our country's history.

TICKETS FOR TWO

My wife Lorraine worked at the St. Lucie County Morningside Library in Port St. Lucie, Florida. Often she used her lunch hour to shop. One lovely spring day in 2006 she finished shopping and was headed back to work. As she backed out of her parking space, another car approached the turn area and she backed into it as it came round the corner. The man got out of his car, as did Lorraine, to view the damage.

To her dismay, the car she backed into was owned by the City of Port St. Lucie and the driver turned out to be a detective from the Port St. Lucie Police Department. He was in plain clothes and called for a road patrol officer to come to the scene. This is normal procedure when a city vehicle is involved in an accident.

After exchanging drivers licenses and registrations it was determined there was only minor damage to the city vehicle and none to Lorraine's car. The officers were very forgiving since the city vehicle had been involved in other minor mishaps in the past. The officer only issued a warning ticket.

* * * *

Four weeks later I drove to Dr. Christian Presutti's office to pick up a prescription for my wife. I was driving south on US1 and made a left-hand turn onto Lyngate Road when I noticed a patrol car behind me with lights flashing. I thought it was headed for the St. Lucie Medical Center. I turned onto Hillmoor Drive and entered the parking lot of the medical building adjacent to the Medical Center. I parked my car and noticed the patrol car was still behind me with lights flashing.

As I exited my vehicle I was approached by an officer of the Port St. Lucie Police Department. We exchanged greeting and he asked me, "Did you see my flashing lights?"

Truthfully I said, "Yes, I thought you were on your way to the St. Lucie Medical Center next door."

Being aware I was a senior driver he asked me, "Do you know why I'm pulling you over?"

I said, "No."

He said, "You ran a red light at the corner of US1 and Lyngate."

I figured he must have been waiting at the corner when I turned off US1. I remained congenial.

He asked me, "Do you have an appointment at the doctor's office?"

I said, "No, I'm only picking up my wife's prescription."

The officer asked me, "Do you know what the fine is for running a red light?"

Again I said, "No."

He said, "It is $87.50, however, I am only going to give you a warning. It will not appear on your driver's license. Just be more careful at intersections in the future."

The tale here is being honest and congenial always pays. (Sometimes a little assistance from the Lord also helps.)

MY IN-LAWS

I have been married to two loving women and am very fortunate to have had two wonderful pairs of in-laws in my lifetime.

My first in-laws, John J. and Catherine Hallahan Flanagan lived in Massachusetts. They were both born in Ireland and migrated to this country prior to World War I where they met. John was born in County Galway in 1890. Catherine was born in County Cork in 1896. They both became citizens of the United States. My father-in-law served in the U.S. Army in France during World War I.

They married in the early 1920's and had two children, Mary Catherine, born in 1922, and John Robert (aka Jack) born in 1924. My father-in-law worked most of his life for the New England Telephone Company retiring before Mary and I were married on October 12, 1957.

Holidays were alternated every other year between my folks in Rochester, New York and Mary's in Springfield, Massachusetts. My father-in-law John died on April 12, 1973 and my mother-in-law Catherine died on January 28, 1986. My first wife, Mary, was very sick at the time and passed away fifteen days later on February 12, 1986.

My second wife Lorraine's parents, Annette Rita and Arthur Raymond La Chance, were also from Massachusetts and had been living at The Willows, an assisted living facility, prior to Ray being placed in a nursing home. Mom was later moved to another assisted living facility in order to be closer to the nursing home.

As a young man, Ray had a bread route and made home deliveries with his truck. In 1936 Ray was employed by the Swank Jewelry Company where he worked for 49 years before retiring in 1985 as their Traffic Manager. He served in the U.S. Army during World War II where his unit was on occupation duty in Japan after the war.

Ray married Annette Bergeron on November 30, 1939. They had five children; Lorraine, Gloria, Ronald, Lillian and Richard. Their home was on Peck Street in Rehoboth, Massachusetts.

Mom had a full-time job raising five children born between 1941 and 1957. She enjoyed pretty clothes, jewelry and family gatherings. Mom and dad enjoyed dancing, singing, and attending National Conventions for Swank.

I did not meet my La Chance in-laws until I started dating their eldest daughter, Lorraine, in the late 1980's. We dated and were married in May of 1993. I retired in 1991 and Lorraine and I traveled to visit them in Massachusetts on many occasions. They also traveled to visit us in Florida.

In January of 2011 Mom was hospitalized with pneumonia and congestive heart failure. She was born in 1920 and was 90 when she died on January 26.

Dad was able to attend her funeral service with members of family and friends who paid their respects at Mom's wake. Two weeks after the funeral Dad La Chance was admitted to the hospital with pneumonia. The children in Massachusetts were at his bedside until his death on February 26, 2011, exactly 30 days after the death of his wife. He had just turned 93 on February 17.

As you can see, the month of January and February are well remembered in the Flanagan, La Chance and Sweeney families.

I have fond memories of these wonderful families.

ON BEING A GENTLEMAN

As I grew up in the 1930's and 40's in the northern part of the United States, my mother tried to instill in me the desire to become a gentleman. Webster's Dictionary defines a gentleman as a man of good family background and social position. It further states he is civilized, educated and sensitive.

I was taught to remove my hat when entering someone's home, a church or an eating establishment. In those days restaurants had a hat check room where you could leave your hat and coat before dining. Other eating establishments had posts attached to their booths with hooks where you could hang your hat and coat. A gentleman removed his hat when entering an elevator, allowing women to go in first and holding the door. You did not use vulgar language in the presence of a female.

Now, in Florida, architects do not design check rooms nor do they provide hat racks in restaurants. I do not know if these facilities are available today up north as I have not been there in the winter months for many years.

Today many gentlemanly actions have become rather lax.

I served in the military during the 1950's. In those days we removed our covers (hats) when entering a building. Guard Duty members of the Military Police wore a Duty Belt and were not required to remove their cover. In combat zones these belts coordinated the military dress. For special ceremonial occasions, such as funerals, memorial services, flag raising events, and weddings, dress uniforms were the proper attire.

Today I have seen seniors and young adults wearing ball caps and hats while eating in nice restaurants. Yes, sometimes my bald head feels the cool effects of air conditioning while dining out, but I still remove my hat.

Maybe I am a little old fashioned, but wouldn't it be nice if in today's society males of all ages would act more gentlemanly and remove their hats when in a restaurant?

A TRIP TO THE CORNER STORE

It was during the early 1950's, after I returned home from the Korean War, that my cousin Lambert Toomey, his wife Jean and their three children (Mary Beth, Mike and Tim) traveled from New Jersey to visit my mother. During their visit there was a need for a few groceries, so my father, cousin Lambert, and his two boys walked a little over 100 yards to Ryans's Red & White Grocery Store at the corner.

On the return trip Tim, the youngest, said to his father, "Tim got to go Poo-poo." Unfortunately, he couldn't wait until we got home and had an accident on the way.

We later learned that the boys had found an open box of Ex-Lax on the dresser in my mother's bedroom. Tim, thinking it was chocolate, ate the "candy" 'cause it "tasted good."

Needless to say, after Tim had his bath and changed his clothes he was the cleanest child in the neighborhood, both inside and out.

TRANSPORTING VETERANS

Early in 1998 I read an article in our newspaper requesting volunteers to drive veterans residing in St. Lucie County, Florida, to the U.S. Veterans Medical Facility in West Palm Beach. I was approved by the Department of Veterans Services for one of these positions. Every day, Monday through Friday, except holidays, free transportation was provided for veterans.

Three 15 passenger vans were purchased by the county, with the assistance from fund raisers by the United Veterans Council. This council consists of approximately 20 veterans' organizations which operate within the area.

Drivers reported at 6:30 a.m. to the county transportation compound in Fort Pierce every morning where they picked up their assigned van and proceeded to the scheduled departure points in Fort Pierce and St. Lucie West.

Veterans were instructed to meet at their designated stations by 7 a.m. and then they were transported to the VA Medical Center. Veterans riding the vans had morning appointments scheduled from 8 a.m. until noon. The return trips of the vans ranged from noon to 2 p.m. getting riders back by mid-afternoon.

In March of 2003, after open heart surgery, I did not drive until I received permission from my doctor in November. Over the past six years I've transported over 1,500 veterans to the VA Hospital while traveling over 33,000 miles back and forth from St. Lucie County to West Palm Beach.

The Board of County Commissioners approved salaries for the van drivers in October of 2002. I continued to drive until late in 2004 when I learned I had macular degeneration. It would become increasingly difficult for me to see, so in the best interest of all concerned I felt it was time to retire from this job.

A STREET OF VETERANS

My parents, Walter and Mary Sweeney, were married in July of 1928. That October they purchased their first and only home on Monroe Parkway in the town of Brighton, New York.

While I was growing up in the 1930's there were four World War I veterans who lived on our street. They were Clarence Hecker, William Perkins, Hobart Owens and my father.

Both Mr. Hecker and Mr. Perkins served with the U.S. Army in France. Both were severely wounded by the German Army.

Mr. Owens served in the U.S. Navy in the submarine division.

My father was a proud U.S. Marine serving his duty at the Parris Island Boot Camp with the Marine Corp Band and was honorably discharged in 1919.

Another neighbor, Ralph Norman, son of Joseph and Gertrude Norman, enlisted in the U.S. Army during the late 1930's. He was assigned to a duty station in Hawaii. He was on duty when the Japanese bombed Pearl Harbor on December 7, 1941. His sister, Eleanor Norman, volunteered and served in the WAVES, a part of the U.S. Navy.

Other Monroe Parkway men, who served in the World War II years, were Joseph Bell Isle, son of our local druggist.

Robert Corbett, son of Hugh and Ethel Corbett, served with the Royal Canadian Air Force.

Richard J Shacter, son of Jack and Molly Shacter, was a member of the Army Air Corps.

Two girls from our street married servicemen during the war. Dorothy Perkins married Charles Reiner and Betty Hart married Richard Wagner. Both of these veterans served in the Army Air Corps and I consider these men a part of Monroe Parkway.

When the Korean War began in June of 1950, I was a member of the U.S. Marine Corps Reserve. Our unit was activated for duty in August of 1950 and by 1951 I was a member of the Fleet Marine Force serving on occupation duty in the Mediterranean. After serving my military duty, I was honorably discharged in May of 1952.

John D. Owens, son of Hobe and Kay Owens, became a member of the U.S. Air Force after graduating from college in the mid 1950's. He was a commissioned officer serving as a Jet Fighter Pilot.

His brother, Donald P. Owens was an ROTC member at the University of Miami. Upon graduation Don became a commissioned officer in the U.S. Air Force from 1960-1965 and served overseas on the isle of Guam.

When my brother, Philip V. Sweeney, completed Grad School in 1958 he was drafted into the U.S. Army in August and served on occupation duty in Germany until July of 1960.

Edward K. Wilson, son of Perry and Helen Wilson, lived on the street from 1934 to the early 1940's. His father was transferred to the greater New York area. After Ed graduated he enlisted in the U.S. Air Force and made the Military his career.

I salute and congratulate all the men and women who served our country in the armed forces. I also want to dedicate this article to my youngest brother, Leo A. Sweeney, who was drafted into the U.S. Army in October of 1959 and served on occupation duty in Korea during the early 1960's. Leo died on Veterans Day, 2009 at the age of 71.

McDONALD'S® COMMUNITY SERVICE AWARD
GENE SWEENEY

Gene Sweeney, this year's recipient of the McDonald's Community Service Award has played a very active role in the Rochester Sports Community.

Gene has been, for the past 35 years, a Sales and Public Relations Representative for The Coca-Cola Company. As such, he has coordinated many programs including the Coke Bleacher Club at Silver Stadium, Section V Basketball Seeding Luncheon, Harvey E. Anderson Scholarship Committee and the United Way Campaign for Coca-Cola. He is the 1985 recipient of the Rochester Press-Radio Club Eddie Meath Community Service Award.

Gene has always felt that giving something back to the community is important. He has accomplished this through his involvement on many committees, such as the Rochester Press-Radio Club, Al Sigl Center Sports Benefit, Rochester Red Wings Baseball Hall of Fame Selection Committee and Greater Rochester Amateur Athletic Federation (a program to assist needy athletes on their quest to become US Olympians).

Gene's other activities include membership in the Monroe County American Legion, Vice-President 2nd Marine Division Association, Fairport Council Knights of Columbus and Egypt Exempt Fireman's Benevolent Association.

ABOUT THE AUTHOR

W. Eugene Sweeney was born and raised in Brighton, New York in the 1930's. Even as a child he cared about his community and signed up for many local organizations. As time went by he often thought of following in his father's footsteps. Walter J. Sweeney served in the United States Marine Corps as a Sergeant. Gene joined the United States Marine Corps Reserve in 1947 and served during the Korean War. After his honorable discharge, he worked for the Rochester Coca-Cola Bottling Co. as Public Relations Director for 35 years.

Gene Sweeney is a past President of the Florida Chapter, 2nd Marine Division Association and a Life Member of the Marine Corps League and the SMDA. He also served 30 years as a volunteer fireman with the Egypt Fire Department in Fairport, NY where he is a past President of the Exempt Club.

Gene was one of the founders of the Greater Rochester Amateur Athletic Federation which raises funds to assist local amateur athletes who have aspirations to compete in the Olympic Games. He also served as a volunteer for the St Lucie County Veterans Services where he drove veterans to the Veterans Hospital in West Palm Beach. He is a life member of the Fourth Degree, Knights of Columbus and American Legion, Post 318 in Port St Lucie, Florida.

His goal is to always help someone and enjoy the trip along the way...

Made in the USA
Charleston, SC
15 August 2016